Love

One Hundred Quotes and Thoughts
With One Hundred Paintings of Lord Krishna

R.N. Kogata • Lalita Kogata

D.K. Printworld (P) Ltd.
New Delhi

First published in India, 2012
ISBN 13: 978-81-246-0617-9
ISBN 10: 81-246-0617-X

A creation of:
Mr R N Kogata & Mrs Lalita Kogata
608, Hiran Magari, Sector-11, Udaipur - India
Phone : +91-94141-58870, +91-294-2583870
e-mail: devkush@rediffmail.com

Published and printed by:
D.K. Printworld (P) Ltd.
"Vedaśrī" F-395, Sudarshan Park
(Metro Station: Ramesh Nagar), New Delhi - 110 015
Phs.: 011-2545 3975, 2546 6019
Fax: 011-2546 5926
e-mail: indology@dkprintworld.com
Web: www.dkprintworld.com

Preface

Love can tell, Love gives courage to suffer, Love gives itself, it is not bought; Love is a beautiful necessity of nature, Love means essentially to give, Love is unconquered in battle, Love conquers all; Love is a gift of God; Love is in beggars as in kings; Love is wiser than ambition; Love teaches how to learn and understand; Love gives two souls a single thought; Love makes two hearts beat as one.

In short, Love has miracle effects.

Both, your verbal as well as written expression of thoughts, needs the excellent ideas to elaborate and illustrate your particular point, to illuminate your imagination and to pose your perfect personality, and that is the aim of this book, whereby, the lovers can express all their feelings in fewer words but with more grace.

This book contains 100 carefully chosen quotations on Love, mixed, modified and created. Some of the thoughts presented are ours, and others are from the people, who have stood by and worked for the values; some were famous names and some others were ordinary people. We have tried to indicate in the acknowledgement page, names of the persons whose quote we have reproduced wherever we could remember. Any amendment/addition in this regard is most welcome from the learned readers.

Krishna is the God of Love and each of the quotes in this book has a painting of Lord Krishna with Radha to inspire you. The paintings alongside quotes, have been created by our professional artists keeping in mind the theme of each individual quote. We sincerely wish that you benefit from these thoughts and pass them on to others you truly love and care for, in order to inspire them to become better and lovely individuals.

Our sincere thanks are due to Antoine De Saint, Arthur Rubinstein, Bruce Lee, Barbara De Angeles, Elbert Hubbard, Henry Miller, Joan Crawford, Karl Menninger, Keiichi Morisata, Leo F Buscaglia, Mark Twain, Maya Angelou, Mignon McLaughlin, Oscar Wilde, Pamela de Roy, Rumi, Soren Kierkegaard, Thomas A Kempis, Zelda Fitzgerald and other eminent writers as also the Holy Bible; who have given such invaluable thoughts to this world.

We prostrate before our parents Smt Kanchan Devi and Shri Bhairav Lal Kogata, and Smt Kamla Devi Nuwal and the late Prof K.M. Nuwal for their benign blessings that have guided us throughout and made us reach the stage where we find ourselves today.

With the expectation of blessings and constructive feedback from all of you.

Lalita and R.N. Kogata

Acknowledgement

Quotations of the following great personalities have been included in this book:

Quote appeared on page no.	*By*
11	Rumi
15	Keiichi Morisata
16	Zelda Fitzgerald
29	Mignon McLaughlin
32	Oscar Wilde
33	Bette Midler
38	Karl Menninger
39	Soren Kierkegaard
40	Antoine de Saint-Exupery
42	Elbert Hubbard
44	Joan Crawford
46	Pamela de Roy
47	Leo F. Buscaglia
48	Leo F. Buscaglia
49	Montaigne

A friend's love says:
If you ever need anything,
I will be there.

True love says:
You will never need anything,
As I am always there!

A very small degree of hope
is sufficient to cause
the birth of love.

There is no remedy for love
but to "love more!"

Absence sharpens love;

Presence strengthens it further!

Bitterness imprisons life,
Love releases it!

Bitterness paralyses life,
Love empowers it!

Bitterness sours life,
Love sweetens it!

Bitterness sickens life,
Love heals it!

Bitterness blinds life,
Love anoints the eyes!

Come out of
the circle of time, and

Come into
the circle of love!

Do you believe in
love at first sight or,
do I have to walk by again?

Don't find love,
let love find you!

That's why it's called
falling in love,
because
you don't force yourself to fall,
you just fall!

Everyone wants to be the sun
that lightens up your life.

But, I would rather be your moon,
so I can shine on you
during your darkest hour
when your sun is not around!

Falling in love with someone
isn't always easy —

Anger… Tears… Laughter…

It is when you want
to be together
despite it all,
that is
when you truly love
each other!

I don't want to live;

I want to love first
and
just live incidentally!

I Love You freely without restrictions,
I Love Your understanding without doubt.
I Love Your honesty without deceit,
I Love You creatively without conditioning.
I Love You now without any reservation,
I Love You physically without pretending.
I Love Your soul without wishing,
I Love Your being without wanting!

I Love You

I sought for love but love ran away from me,

I sought my soul but my soul I couldn't see;

Then I sought you, and I found all the three!

I would rather be hated
for who I am, than be loved
for who I am not!

If I could rearrange
the alphabets,

I would put
'U' and 'I'
together!

If I were to be anything in this world . . .
I'd be your tears!!! . . .

So, I can be conceived in your heart,
born in your eyes,
live on your cheeks
and die on your lips!!!

If love hurts,
then love some more;

If love hurts some more,
then love even more;

If love hurts even more . . .
then love till it hurts no more !!!

If love were to be taxed,

I would wish to be,

the highest tax payer!

If smiles were water, I would give you the sea,
If holding hands was a second, I would give you hours!
If hugs were leaves, I would give you a tree,
If a kiss was a raindrop, I would give you showers!
If you loved a planet, I would give you a galaxy,
And if love is life, I will give you mine!

If the only possible way,
we can be together, is in my dreams,
then I will sleep forever!

If you have love,
you don't need to have anything else;

If you don't have it,
it doesn't matter much, what else you have!

If you love somebody
then let them go.

If they return,
they were always yours;

And, if they don't,
they never were!

In my life
I learned
how to love, to smile,
to be happy, to be strong,
to work hard, to be honest,
to be faithful and to forgive:

but, I could not learn
how to stop
remembering you!

In the arithmetic of love —

One plus one
equals everything,

Two minus one
equals nothing!

It breaks your heart to see,
the one you love,
is happy with someone else.

But it's more painful to know
that the one you love,
is unhappy with you!

It is wrong to think
that love comes from
long companionship
and persevering courtship.

Love is the offspring
of spiritual affinity and
unless that affinity is
created in a moment,
it will not be created
for years or even generations!

Keep love in your heart;
A life without it
is like a sunless garden,
where the flowers are dead!

The consciousness of
loving and being loved
brings warmth and
richness to life
that nothing else can bring!

Let the world stop turning,
Let the sun stop burning.
Let them tell me
Love is not worth going through!
If it all falls apart
I will know deep in my heart.
The only dream that
Mattered, had come true;
In this life,
I was loved by you!

Life without love

is like barren a tree,

without blossom or fruit!

Love —

- is all in fire
  yet is ever freezing.
- is much in winning
  yet is more in losing.
- is ever sick
  yet is never dying.
- is ever true
  yet is ever lying.
- does dwell in liking
  is mad in loathing.
- love indeed is everything
  yet indeed is nothing!

Love –

- alone can tell.
- ceases to be pleasure, when it ceases to be a secret.
- gives courage to suffer.
- is the only glimpse we are permitted of eternity.
- gives itself, it is not bought.
- is a beautiful necessity of the beautiful nature.
- is the noblest frailty of the mind.
- means essentially to give.
- is unconquered in battle.
- conquers all.
- is a gift of God.
- is love, in beggars as in kings.
- is wiser than ambition.
- is love's reward.
- teaches how to learn and understand.
- gives two souls a single thought.
- makes two hearts beat as one.

Love at first sight
may be all right,

but, it might be wise
to take a second look!

Love cures people:

Both
the ones who give it
and
the ones who receive it!

Love does not
alter the beloved,

it alters itself!

Love
does not contain
in gazing at each other,
but
in looking together
in the same direction!

Love fails,
only when
we fail to love!

Love grows by giving.

The love we give away
is the only love we keep.

The only way to retain love
is to give it away!

Love
is a condition of the mind
at a time
when
the mind is
out of condition.

Love is a fire!
But whether it is
going to warm your heart
or burn down your house
you can never tell!

Love is a little word,
you can make it big!

Love is a wonderful thing.

You never have to take it away
from one person
to give it to another.

There is always
more than enough
to go around.

Love is always bestowed
as a gift freely, willingly
and without expectation.

Don't love to be loved.
Love to love!

Love is always open arms.

If you close your arms about love
you will find
that you are left holding
only yourself!

Love is life!
and if you miss love,
you miss life!!

Love is like a friendship
caught on fire.

In the beginning
a flame very pretty
often hot and fierce
but still only light
and flickering.

As love grows older
our hearts mature
and our love becomes
as coals deep-burning
and unquenchable.

Love is not how long
you have been together;

Not how much
you have given or received;

Not how many times
you have helped each other;

It is how you value each other!

Love is not how you forget
but how you forgive;

not how you listen
but how you understand;

not what you see
but what you feel;

and not how you let go
but how you hold on!

Love is patient, love is kind,
It does not envy, it does not boast,
It is not proud, it is not rude,
It is not self-seeking,
It is not easily angered,
It keeps no record of wrongs,
Love does not feel the burden,
Love thinks nothing of trouble,
Love does not delight in evil
But rejoices with the truth!

It always protects, always trusts,
always hopes and always perseveres.
Though weary, it is not tired,
Though pressed, it is not straitened,
Though alarmed, it is not confounded,
Love never fails!

Love is the only force
capable of
transforming an enemy
into a friend!

Love is the only thing
you cannot have
until you give it away!

Love knows no reasons.
Love knows no lies.
Love defies all reasons.

Love has no eyes.
But love is not blind.

Love sees,
But doesn't mind!

Love life
and life will
love you back!

Love people
and they will
love you back!

Love one another
and you will be happy.

It is
as simple and as difficult
as that!

Love puts the fun in together.

The sad in apart.

The "hope" in tomorrow.

The "you" in the heart!

Love recognizes no barriers;

It jumps hurdles, leaps fences,
penetrates walls
to arrive at its destination,
full of hope!

Love rules
without rules!

Love the heart that hurts you,

but never hurt the heart that loves you!

Love unlocks doors
and opens windows
that were not even
there before!

Love,
like a river,
will cut a new path
whenever it meets an obstacle!

Love,
like paint,
can make things beautiful
when you spread it,

but
it simply dries up
when you don't use it!

Loving you
could take my life,

but when I look into your eyes,
I know
you are worth that sacrifice!

Being deeply loved
by someone
gives you strength

while loving someone deeply
gives you courage!

Maybe God wants us
to meet a few wrong people
before meeting the right one,

so that when we finally
meet the person,
we will know,
how to be grateful?

My love for you
is a journey —

starting at forever
and ending at never!

Never look for beauty,
it will fade one day.

Never look for good skin,
it will grow old one day.

But look for a loyal heart,
which will miss you everyday.

No love,
No happiness.

Know love,
Know happiness!

No one is worth your tears
and the only one who is,
will never make you cry!

Nothing beats love
at first sight
except love with insight!

Once, I knew you…
Often, I miss you…
Always, I will care for you…
Never, will I forget you…

Because I never want to lose
someone as special as you!

One day you will ask me:
What is more important to you —
me or your life?

I will say
my life,
and you will go and leave
without even knowing
that you are my life!

Perfect love is rare indeed. For, to be a lover will require that you continually have —

- the subtlety of the very wise,
- the flexibility of the child,
- the sensitivity of the artist,
- the understanding of the philosopher,
- the acceptance of the saint,
- the tolerance of the scholar and
- the fortitude of the certain!

Person like you, is found
only once in a lifetime.

That is why, I want you
to take care of yourself
because I don't want
to spend another lifetime
looking for another
person like you!

Sea is never large,
but sight of our viewing is larger.

No one's Love is lesser
but our expectations are higher!

Some people like to paint trees,
I like to paint love.

I find it more meaningful
than painting trees!

The loneliest place
in the world is
human heart, when
love is absent!

The most important thing
a father can do for his children
is to love their mother!

The one thing
we can never get enough of,
is love;

and the one thing
we can never give enough of,
is love!

The person who tries to live alone
will not succeed as a human being.

His heart withers if it does not
answer another heart.

His mind shrinks away if he hears
only the echoes of his own thoughts
and finds no other inspiration.

The ultimate test of
a relationship is to disagree
but to hold hands!

Three grand essentials to happiness
in this life, are —

Something to do,
Something to love and
Something to hope for!

Time is —
Too slow for those who wait.
Too swift for those who fear.
Too long for those who grieve.
Too short for those who rejoice.
But for those who love,
Time is eternity!

To get the full value of joy,
you must have someone to share it with!

To love a person
is to learn the song
that is in their heart,
and then to sing it to them
when they have forgotten!

To love is nothing,

To be loved is something.

But —

To be loved by the one you love
is everything!

To the whole world,
you may be just one person,
but to me you are
the whole world!

Trouble is a part of your life,
if you don't share it,
you don't give the person
that loves you, enough
chance to love you enough!

True love begins,
when nothing is
looked for in return!

True love doesn't consist of
holding hands,

it consists of binding hearts!

True love doesn't have
a happy ending;

True love doesn't have
an ending!

True love is like ghosts,
which everybody talks about
but only few have seen!

We waste time looking
for the perfect lover,
instead of creating
the perfect love!

What holds you together
is far greater than
what can tear you apart!

What is the difference
between pleasure and torture?

Pleasure is thinking of you,
and torture is thinking of you too much!

When I saw you I was afraid to meet you.
When I met you I was afraid to touch you.
When I touched you I was afraid to love you.
Now that I love you, I am afraid to lose you!

Who do you turn to, when
the only person in the world
that can stop you from crying,
is exactly the one making you cry?

Women admire a man
because he is strong,
but they love him
for his weaknesses!

You can always get someone
to love you —
even if you have to do it yourself!

You can give
without loving.

But you can't love
without giving!

You love because you weep.
You weep because you hurt.
You hurt because you fail.
You fail because you try.
You try because you need.
You need because you want.
You want because you feel.
You feel because you live.
You live because you love!

You never lose
by loving,

You always lose
by holding back!

A song is not a song
until you sing it.

A bell is not a bell
until you ring it.

Love is not love
until you give it!